# Mor(e)

# Mor(e)

more than motherhood

Ruth Rostrup

Mor is the Norwegian word for Mother

but in a land and life that's foreign to me
estranged ears turn the name from a noun to a call

Do more                                          Experience more
Give more                                             Have more
Be more                      You are more

You are not enough                               You are everything

and I find my home
in the spine that holds both sides together.

All the pages of a life we fruitlessly try to translate
and the meaning we gain from faithfully attempting anyway.

This is not a self-help book.
This book won't tell you what to do.

This is just a book full of messages
dedicated to you,

for a time when it can feel like no one sees you at all

- but I do.

Read me how you want

Take what you need

# Pages on the left
# are stories shared.

The dark days.

The days often left unsaid
left behind
left in a body
by those that would rather forget.

But here we are,
sharing her between our hands instead.

# Pages on the right
# are stories needed.

From the other side.

The words I craved back then
in the days that never felt right
and, if I'm being honest,
still don't
sometimes.

Our journeys aren't linear,
so spend time on whichever side speaks to you.

Open me up on random pages
or read me section by section.

This was created for you.

So savour, explore
and take any meaning that you need.

Contents

# Labour

Some people split their life
in to before and after
a child is born.

Mine was torn
the day I lost myself.

And like in the pages of a familiar book,
we find our answers
we find our balance

we find ourselves again.

We find home.

I relive that day
every night since.
A wound put into words
stuck on repeat.

I live in its re-telling
and labour on and on.

I drown in the echos
of my old body,
my old self,
lost at sea.

I'm not looking back,
I'm looking in.
Towards the girl
who went through it all.

The innocent,
the bright-eyed,
the worthy girl

who I promise
I won't ever leave behind again.

I'm taped
to a horror-house carousel,
spinning faster and faster,
blurring all that's real around me.


I try to focus on the dazzling, hot flashes
of the parts of my life that once were.


My people,
and their stories
that once filled with colour
the pages of my own

are whipped and torn away
as I spin and spin
over and over
over and over
over and over

clinging to this one last tale,
the last place I was ever known.

She is flawed
She is cringey
She is erratic
She is clumsy
She is sad
She is worn
She is bitter
She is patchy

She is fucked up
but this is the story
and now she's mine.

# "WELCOME TO THE BEST DAY OF YOUR LIFE."

strung hurriedly to all the rooms in our minds.
IV streamers, gaslit balloons
paint the cracks with artificial, sickening syrup
in pinks and blues.


At the door, we'll inject our faces with Instagram filters
'cus God forbid we show
that when we turn up to the best day of our lives
it's grief
not joy
wrapped up in wholesale plastic bows.

And when I learned to love her
I could let her go.

I didn't go into labour that day.
My whole life has been in labour.

A woman's work is never done.

I don't know if sharing
will help anybody else
but it might save me
and I'm worth saving too.

From the first contraction,
          time changed entirely.

    I saw it squeezed,
              and s t r e t c h e d into an infinite ocean,

                    devastatingly dark.


And as each wave battered us both,

      I went further adrift


                          taking the pain from the surface
to protect the spectators
on my shore.


          Moving my body,
                    like waves,
  as the sands of my reality washed  a
                            w
                                  a
                                    y


never to be returned again.


Not even now.

She has wild hair with a rhythm she can't keep pace.
She's the best listener but forgets her own PIN codes most days.
She makes little cringe noises,
remembering awkward things at night.
She's still afraid of the dark but loves the evenings when it's big and
open and hers. She needs to cry and laugh in equal measures.
She builds the best piers to harbour yours.
She loves to make you laugh purely because
she loves to make you laugh.
She's an immigrant in many ways,
more and less than she would like.
She was born into Newton's cradle of dysfunction and divergents.
She creates order from chaos, everywhere but her.
She would do anything for you...except send text messages when
you want her to. She built an electric guitar in woodwork class,
sanded it down to perfection that she never played.
She picked up a bow and arrow in her thirties
because it's what she wanted at thirteen.
She writes and resolves in work, in play, in all the things,
every day.
She fell in love and learned to ride a bike three times.
She then took on the son and the snow
and sat higher than she ever had.
She inhales music like a withdrawn smoker, blurring her vision in
the volume, says she's a metal girl at heart
but it's the sad songs that keep her alive.
She thinks heaven is a balcony sunset with wine and tapas
and you.
She loves the smell of fresh basil.
She welcomes age but fears the time and needs some help coming
back to now, where she's safe,
she's still here
and she's mine.

Close the door,
bunker down,
clench my fists,
claw my thighs,


pain unfolds and I squash it down.


squash it down.


squash it down.


God forbid I make a sound.

Every woman
has a daughter
that deserves to be raised up
from the inside.

How are you talking to her?

i don't want to impose.

But I knew that time had come for me.
For us.

What the mind cannot reconcile
the body will always speak

and every cell of mine
cried out to bring this child.


My heart knew their face
long before
and brought them to life in my dreams.

My body knew this place
from before
generations of pain bursting out through my seams.

"It's happening!" I cry

"No, it's not" they reply

"I need help" I cry

"No, you don't" they reply

"Wait longer" they reply

"It is time" I cry

Taped to a horror-house carousel,
these are the words
played to mothers
on repeat.

This is my first child, not my first body.

I go where I'm told;
but it's abandoned,

empty.

I haul swollen feet
on restless legs
towards open faces,
sturdy hands
and warm voices
but I'm met,
instead,
with
endless
dark
corridors
filled with scattered, disjointed beds.

Signs I can't read.
I don't understand.

Where are the people?
Where are my people?

We light each other's torches
but we do not carry them.

Another whip-crack hits.

We sway back and forth
to smooth the sharp edges of pain
from down

down

down

Bears trapped in cages,
pacing back and forth.

Storm clouds bulge over the horizon
and stalk towards our midnight home.

Enveloped in the hot, viscous atmosphere
the hair on my arms and neck cut through the thick air
standing tall to meet the alert
of the danger at our threshold.

But I do not flinch.

My limbs are wrapped around his newborn nest,
creating a cave of our own

and in the haze of it all
I become suddenly aware
- and still remember now -
the first time I felt fully tuned in
and utterly fearless.

The fresh and fleeting storm
shows up naively to my mother nature.

The unfeigned, carnal creature that I am.

I would chase away the thunder with my roar
and pound mountains in to sand

- the world folds in on itself and retreats to the sea at my stare.

Wise enough to fear
but I fear nothing for you.

Waan soo wada marnay

Na de geboorte voel je een
explosie van liefde

Ser mamá no se mide por lo
que dejas atrás al tener un
bebé, sino por lo que ganas
al hacerlo

Nårh, så er dit liv nok over

Genieße es solange sie so
klein sind, es geht alles so
schnell - du wirst schon
sehen

дети - это счастье
дальше будет проще

Iedere    moeder    kan
borstvoeding geven als ze
dat wil

Det ordner seg nok, skal du
se. Det er bare å ta tiden
til hjelp.

Ciesz się, inni mają gorzej.

How long do they expect us to walk these same corridors?

Following signs that don't make sense.

I burned holes
in most parts of my life
with a magnifying glass
and it wasn't until I saw
I'd never understand it all
I realised the sun had set.

Lie back,
open legs,
look away.

A stranger's hand enters
to  s c r a p e  in a seed of shame.


Flick the switch,
shut off from that body.

How easy.


A gift from our foremothers
and we thank them
with burning,
solemn,
silent tears.

the knowing
between women
we speak a story aloud
and exchange another in silence
a language of the eyes
of the hands
the tugging of sleeves
the drawing of energy
the intuition
the vibe
the knowing.
The knowing of the truth between all the truths we speak.

Centimeter by centimeter.
I feel powerful.

Centimeter by centimeter.
It will be the last time.

Centimeter by centimeter.
All by myself.

Centimeter by centimeter.
Milestones only understood
by those who were made to climb.

Centimeter by centimeter.
They didn't believe me when I said it was happening.

It won't be the last time.

I used to care about conquering it all
but the view from the warmth of my basecamp
never looked and felt
so good.

High on adrenaline
from the progress that I made.

The view is good from up here.
But it's not enough.
It's never enough.
It's never enough.
It's never enough.
It's never enough.
It's never enough.
It's never enough.
It's never enough.
It's never enough.
It's never enough.
It's never enough.
It's never enough.
It's never enough.
It's never enough.
It's never enough.
It's never enough.
It's never enough.
It's never enough.

I say when.
to breathe
to hold
to run
to cry
to jump
how high
to swing
to the sky
I look
to see
to grasp
to fall
and breathe.
I say when.

I pack my bags
with music,
scent
and colour

only to tuck it all away
in a far and hidden corner.

Out of the way
from the life tasks at hand.

Embarrassed
that I had the audacity
to make my joyful, lavender plans.

Let it grow.
A thousand needles in my arm
set the tree ablaze
purple, blue, green, on satin.
Stain it red, stain it red.
A sudden calm inside my head.

We are art, I wear mine on my sleeve.

I'm surrounded by strong women.
Hair swept back for the task,
sublime wrinkles crown their eyes,
and with divine, diverse tongues,
their song of knowing is spun.


I want
so, so badly
to soak up their power

like a tree propping up a monsoon sky
that secretly longs for the sun.

But I'm bloated,
roots bursting and rotten with water,
and I'm starting to shut down.

I don't blame the heroes
for not knowing,
as they pluck the babe from the water

that           river           could
        the            itself           drown.

We fill up on sunshine

but our roots develop in the dark.

"Do you want pain relief?" they ask

But what I hear is

## "Do you want help?
## "Do you want rest?"
## "Do you want to be taken care of?"

I am so sick of mistranslations.

I know
how anger rises in the child
who isn't able to speak
not fully
not yet

how the desire cascades into desperation
and frustration into anger which is fear
fear that no one will ever hear them
not really
not ever.

I know
because I'm still learning too
and cascading all the same

I know
now too
what it means to be seen
when you can't be heard
not alone
not fully
not ever.

In my space, my home, in my patience, my alone,
things progress exactly as they should.
I happen.


Now we labour and analyse.
Forcing the   shift,
           grind
           and push
to make things work
in ways we think they should.


And everything stops.


We're stuck.


Our body shuts down,
carrying a heart
squeezed under the weight
of where we think we want to be.

To be absolutely clear,
this is not an advertisement for home births.

My home is a safe space now.

I have written
and rewritten
the feeling of that hospital gown
so many times.

It lives as a **heaviness** on my shoulders,
*rot* in my nose
and a *sickness* on my skin.

It's my grief to live in
so I'll at least make it beautiful.

Tied up in wires,
taped and pierced
with needles
into bruises from veins,
like a child's, too small.
Over
and over
and over
and over.

Skin  stretche  d,
     b  u  rn e d
a nd   to rn.


It's
so
hard
to
move.


yet "MOVE" they demand.

Go buy yourself those flowers
and put them in every room
of your home.

Bathe yourself in texture.

Light candles that dance
in a show
just for you.

I move from the bed,
to the floor,
gripping straps,
inflated ball.
The circus elephant is on parade.
I make a joke,
they laugh
politely.


They offer up an old wooden stool with a hole
                                    a child's potty (retch),
and a hospital walker
                            for the infirm (gag).


Humiliated.
I make a joke,
no one laughs.

I wasn't put on this Earth to be anything for anyone.
To be glamorous
To be gallant
To be graceful.
Grace is not where my power lies.


These bones are made of granite
around a stack of molten coals
ancient vines twist and pull
a rugged old oak spine.


This mother's nature reeks of peat and heat and hurricanes.


Now watch as I move mountains.

We (I) work and we wait.

In her I trust.

In the girl who completed her tasks diligently in class, through uterus pains shown only in white knuckles around seat edges she clasped.

In her I trust.

In her I trust.

In the girl who was taught she was never enough, that any cries for help would be making a fuss so she learned to hug herself in and bolster herself up.

In her I trust.

In her I trust.

In the girl who stepped up to fill the gaps of the parent estranged and learned to subdue the other with the performance that a perfect daughter could never lapse.

In her I trust.

In her I trust.

In the woman who had to choose between milk and bread after 12 hour shifts, relying on herself to be fed and now she rests her bones in her own secure, stable bed.

In her I trust.

In her I trust.

In the woman who learned to put herself first, above all else, she would never again become immersed into people and projects and places where she felt coerced.

In her I trust.

In her I trust.

In the woman who got up and ran when she needed to run and seized every prize that she resolved must be won and stopped when she decided that she was done.

In her I trust.

In her I trust.

I crave sharp wit
to cut my mind free of itself,
shared quips that make eyes twinkle.

To be reminded of the very human,
soulful,
female strength that I have,

that I need right now.

The people in your space
hold a mirror up to you,
to show you
who
you
are.

Who you can be
for yourself.

SHAME SHAME SHAME SHAME SHAME
SHAME SHAME SHAME SHAME SHAME
SHAME SHAME SHAME SHAME SHAME
SHAME SHAME SHAME SHAME SHAME
SHAME SHAME SHAME SHAME SHAME
SHAME SHAME SHAME SHAME SHAME
SHAME SHAME SHAME SHAME SHAME
SHAME SHAME SHAME SHAME SHAME
SHAME SHAME SHAME SHAME SHAME
SHAME SHAME they had me SHAME SHAME
SHAME SHAME expose my chest SHAME SHAME
SHAME SHAME and fondle myself SHAME SHAME
SHAME SHAME to a silent audience. SHAME SHAME
SHAME SHAME i let out a sob. SHAME SHAME
SHAME SHAME no one reacted. SHAME SHAME
SHAME SHAME SHAME SHAME SHAME
SHAME SHAME SHAME SHAME SHAME
SHAME SHAME SHAME SHAME SHAME
SHAME SHAME SHAME SHAME SHAME
SHAME SHAME SHAME SHAME SHAME
SHAME SHAME SHAME SHAME SHAME
SHAME SHAME SHAME SHAME SHAME
SHAME SHAME SHAME SHAME SHAME

**sexual assault**

**noun**

**Definition of sexual assault**

: illegal sexual contact that usually involves force upon a person without consent or is inflicted upon a person who is incapable of giving consent (as because of age or physical or mental incapacity) or who places the assailant (such as a doctor) in a position of trust or authority

Merriam-Webster. (n.d.). Sexual assault. In Merriam-Webster.com dictionary. Retrieved October 29, 2021, from https://www.merriam-webster.com/dictionary/sexual%20assault

I lock eyes on those ceiling tiles
and I push.

Can you imagine
what our ceilings would scream
if they could.

Having met the stare of so many women
who failed in helping her body,
so forced it instead.

I push and I push and we push.

"Good girl" they say "Give us more."

I push away my whole body.


        I live within four
        white plasterboards,
        hundreds of tiny
        indents, parallel
        plastic lines, a smoke
        detector.

We walked to the swingset above the city
you'd swear the chains would reach
the other side of the fjord
and in winter afternoons
that were night
those chains could release you to the stars.

My kid isn't scared
like I was back then.
I was always worried I'd go too far
my organs didn't seem to want to fly that high
as high as the others
as high as maybe I would've liked to go.

But now
after his turn,
it's mine.
I push off the loop of those chains
and further
and float into the Milky Way sky.

I exist
and disappear

in a weightless abandon
of restraint.

I push    until my face fills to bursting with water.
I push    until my eyes tear red.
I push    until my nose bleeds
and nothing exists but the nightmare in this bed.

Every minute is an hour
and
        the
            hours
                disappear
                    into
                        endless
                            more
                                horizons.

I
take
my
middle
finger
and
draw
a
line
in
the
sand
so
deep
all
but
the
moon
topples
down
in
to
the
fateful
shining
NiFe

# "Push!"

So I push until I have no more to give.
For hours.

# "More!"

No amount of words,
across any number of pages
could take their minds into the depth of time
these traumas trap us in.
A foreverness spoken on the level of the soul.

We would have to drag a part of them in there with us
and leave it there forever, too.

In those few hours I experienced eternity.
A year is not enough to process that
A lifetime
A generation
A lineage

I knew
from a previous life
not to take things lying down

I knew.

And we never fucking forget it.

I have no more
words, no more
feelings, no body,
no more.
Only ceiling tiles.

I staple "wanted" posters to all the trees

My pursuit for her will bring forests to their knees

I breathe in
and hold the colour green
until the grief and pain and all is crystal clear.

I breathe out the dusty knowledge

                  that she's been lost
                  for years.

Waves of siren songs
echo down on to my lonely little sailboat
to lead me further into exhaustion
with tantalising hope

but their calls ripple right through me.

"You can do this."
I'm already done.
"You're so strong"
I'm fading away.
"It's nearly over"
No it's not.

What did I do to deserve such kindness?
What did I do to deserve such torture?

But the trap behind the tune always reveals itself:
"Push. More. Give us more!"

It doesn't matter anyway. I'm done. I'm gone.
Nobody, no more.

"I've learned that people will forget what you said, people will forget what you did, but people will never forget how you made them feel."–
Maya Angelou


In the midst and mist of it all
where I remembered so little
someone grabbed me
a midwife I think
or a nurse
I don't know
and said something powerful
to me
but I'm not totally sure what

but what I do remember was

Her foreignness like mine
The angry, on my behalf, look in her eyes
Her claw grip on my shoulders
The way she looked so intently at me
The welcomed audacity to shake me a little
The yell
that was a whisper
that was a plea.

Years later
there are days that grip on my shoulders pulls me forward
and the echo of those roaring eyes helps me focus mine

I was told something powerful that day
an unspoken lesson I can't remember but I'll never forget.

My face is still now,
but not like theirs.


Calmness is a living quiet.
My stillness is a lacking.

And then the lacking turned into space
and that space dropped into silence
        a silence that I longed for
        for so, so long
and I laid down in that place
        a dark place where I knew I couldn't belong

and that silent place became my limbo
        between a breath and a death
and that breath became another
and another
and another.

I'm eight years old, lying
on top of a plastic storage
container at the side of
my house. Chaos and
yelling saturate the brick
touching the back of my
hand. I fill my lungs with
cool, sparkling, dusk air
and soak up every tiny kiss
of rain until the opening
sky forces me back inside,
in to the house, away from
home - Jungle in a glass box,
my grandad's beard, tomato
plants twice my height,
warm lungs - The smell
of fresh basil - Trapped in
the bathroom at school,
girls kick and slam on the
door and fill my throat
with heartbeats and tears
- Sawdust. My own room
imagined and re-imagined
a hundred times - Midnight
in Greece, Jessica's feet
rippling the watery stars
- A scratchy, bottle-green
jumper - Fairy cups made
with delicate flowers and
filling them with potions.
A little girl's secret garden
tea party by the road, the
world trembles as a huge
double-decker bus roars by
and all I see is -

My mother's face.
My mother's face.
My mother's face.

Breath leaves me in a sigh that takes my muscles with it.
I am released.


And I fall

I fall back back into a shrunken, shriveled body,
a body relinquished
but not relieved.


Back

but not really


back to a room buzzing with people.

I stepped into the light
I saw the other side

Came face to face with The Truth.

Do you want to know what I saw?

A mirror.

Reflecting back the life we live

and leave in search of more.

Flooded with sights and sounds.
A blanket of flesh thrown over me.
A baby is born
in exchange for a piece of the woman
lost forever in the ceiling tiles.

Everyone's relief is **palpable**.

You'd think
recovery would be full
of cushions and quiet
tears in your tea
gentle hands on your shoulder
the slow snuggle down
into the place you need to be.

But mine came at me
in blasts of dizzy fever.
I retch between desperate breaths
and hurl the content of my body
through itself
pound my fists on the ground
water them with ugly wretched sobs.
**Acid.**
**Followed by acid**
**followed by acid**
until it's all burned away
but the acid keeps on coming.

Thankfully.

I look down towards my heart,
Iver.
His name means eagerness for life
and he cries ferociously to claim it.
Iver.
I don't recognise him clearly yet.
It will be quite a while before I do.

I cannot meet your energy
but I'll forever be the home
you come back to
whenever you need to replenish it.

"I did it"

I shoot for strength and revelry
but my tongue is slick thick
with the cries for help that never made it out.

Years of them.

aplfhoendøægkbavcufljrbsmj
dbbsjfoeuabkfprugwbamcåjhav
wuitljavduabvfuoptnvzcreutol
abdhjfirhabajlfnavgaidlgøjegau
oeWeorhavhwjråahavabfncggf
awgfrrææaheironavcrukanrmg
hujoishrbjelaloselcjebyitlambe
gryilliabchejktlkabcbrkthbauci
rhbvakføajagayuwråäahaveuro
kcbvayeirljgvsjfoutgabjckfluae
hourselvesetbnckaliuabfjtinbk
ahbsytiæajagvxcvtyurotoiahan
dbvfruirokahbzvuiøføahgfeuyi
ejlajhvayslfjhbauverløøaaghvd
bvcyruekmabayucleuygrvbhja
kjxfnjanbdbgfyiroiutehhkamn
bsearchcvyiouthjkanbdvcbaku
ygetæageutosoaåauegrtjmabbb
vjuuwgwofiiskdhrhbbtmamoc
hfuoauhebnbtklanbxhjltiuhabc
jhkrøuhtbkancjb,jhtiaøæzjhbd
vvayqieoerjhqbqbhrlihbachuro
ithjkanjbxbhfoijthajkanbdbvvh
thejfoiuahebtjkflkjahusoijvjtbj
kasuhthhkalkbxhjgltiuhtwæaih
agetbhmamnzbjkcxhiuhuhruh
whøajuhdbjkøcjabbdhjtriuhab
nxmnhbbuvoiperfecturhahjhb
abvchjiuhajkanhbxdbyfrkuhab
absmhbcbjxkjhahrhutkjabnbs
bwordsklajherhkachjlrhbabchj
rjhsfhrioæåakherhjaljrhtbkaløa
khgdfuancjb,jhtiaepojwølsjefn

I fucking did it.
I made it out through the other side.
It's over.
I'm alive.
I can breathe.
I can rest.

                                        If only

                                  I could just

                            reach in and find

                          the little girl lost

                          and bring her too.

This summer I took her to the stationery store
the really fancy one in that trendy part of town
where the walls are brimming but the room is so quiet
and curated perfectly
for creatives
just like her
and I gave her all the time in the world
watched her allow herself
to reach out and caress every notebook
the cool leathers
the orange suede
she opened each one
and soaked up the feeling of each blank page
tumbling papers
the sensation of waves of potential
tantalising her hands and her feet at the beach.
When she asked about money
I told her that's taken care of
it's not her job to worry about that
not now
Instead she should worry about the red or the blue
and if the pen should match
revel in the detail of the decisions
enjoy that glittery giddyness
I thought only a child could have
but when her eyes widened
and her heart filled
and her lungs became drenched in abundance
so did mine
I started to take her everywhere with me
my inner child
and me, combined.

They take away my baby.

And there is still more they want of me.

"The placenta is still inside."
"You need to push more."

It's not enough.
It's not over.

It's never going to be over.

Looking back
the biggest certainty I took
into my motherhood
came from my father

a lesson about being enough
a lesson I had to unlearn

and when you don't remove those parts of yourselves
even the parts you used to love
they will corrode
and fester
and poison you.

I goddamn fucking push.
To this day I don't know how.

To this day I don't know how
all the books and movies and fuck-off bloggers
make it out like it's all about that one moment
when the hard work pays off
when you've earned your rest and joy.

> To this day I don't know how.
> To this day I'm still learning to stop pushing.

The master archer

knows when

and how to let go.

Doctors shove the midwives aside.

The once worshipped body

                                    first home to us all.
                    Tenderly carried and cared for:
        Fragrant oils, yoga, three heartbeats under cotton bedsheets,
                    caressed with wishful, reverent hands.
                        The wall between us and everything

becomes the flesh we reject.


The miracle life giver is a poison,
a threat,
a boundary that must be removed.

Remove me.

I went
to the dreamiest hotel
set right on the edge of the Norwegian wild.
Walked there to the steady beat
of one heart, that was mine.
The quiet carried my sails
all the way
to the boundless sky.

The table cloths
like the bedsheets
were perfect snow white
and cooled my parallel skin
like oasis springs
in an endless summer time.

God,
the food.
Every bite an exhibition
just for one.
I sat and savoured
the scenes and the wine
until every drop was soaked up and gone.

The only audience was the reverent forest
in my native retreat of one.

When did they stop looking at me?

The greatest gift.

A tearful hug
as she whispers "I know"
which really means
I feel.

I feel, in part, your pain
and I'll take it away with me.
So you can fill this moment with whatever gifts you need.

But there is none better than this,
dear friend,
a tearful hug with "I know"
that pushes away the whole world in this moment
and allows me simply to be seen.

More bodies
more shoving
more pushing, pushing, pushing.

But that's all down there,
down in the reeds.

Here I am floating above it all.
Lost forever amongst the ceiling tiles.

Don't look for me.

There's a child that needs to be held.

Yes, I lost her
but I'll wait.

I see your steady, caring hands pappa
but your eyes give away the small boy soul.
There aren't enough hands in the world to carry these broken men.

The great fall
        - together.

The beams of our houses will erode away
someday
you know.

Our clothes will fill the earth
until they don't
anymore.

Wedding rings will line the bellies of whales
that cast shadows over airports
and churches
all the same.

All these things
we build
will inevitably crumble

and
we
will
fall

                so let's
                at least
                fall
                together.

The doctor reaches inside of me
as deep as she can go
and offers me a pain I can't refuse.

She grasps at my insides (no metaphors here).

They can't leave anything behind.
They won't leave anything behind.

I hid my secrets.

I hid what I needed to

inside of my endpapers.

Marbled my maps in rich emeralds, maroons and blue.
Oh that blue.
You've never seen a blue like that
until I open the covers
and reveal it to you.

A century-old wail of pain leaves my body again
"STOP!"
The body asks for what it needs even when we cannot
"STOP!"
The biggest con in a word that women have ever been taught
"Please.
God.
Stop."

Through women's mouths the universe calls out.
And the world
pushes
through
those
words
like
stone
through
snow.

RUTH ROSTRUP

# AVA

# LAN

# CHE

I shake my head
appalled by my own demands for boundaries.

How dare I.

> "I know. I know.
> I'm sorry"

I'm sorry for causing a fuss
said every woman
as they merely asked for peace.

No more.

The hand reaches further.

How deep is my body to have given so much

and still gives now.

I do what I'm asked.

Even when they ask for too much.

I offer myself as flesh on a plate.

It's all I have left,

so I guess I'll give that too.

The hangman
gave me more hope
and comfort
than any line of poetry
or well-meaning piece of advice
or care.

In the hangman's lack of hope
I saw that I too must learn to let go.

To feel my despair
and all of the things
in the end of days
and to accept that I am there anyway.

Then, in the stillness
after the struggle
I'll learn to see things in a whole new way -

In these temporary moments
dangling on the rope

        - between my existence before and after.

The hangman's greatest gift to us all
is his perspective.

A gush
A flood
A rush of blood to the floor.
Life-giving flesh leaves me forever

                                                          (never again)

The last piece of a united us is gone

                                              (or so I thought)


and with it blood
so much blood.
You asked for more. So here it is you fuckers. Bleed me dry.


                Take

every

                                        last


                    drop


                                              of



                                      her.

Go on then.
Take my everything.
Empty me out.

And I'll fill up,
unwavering eyes, unflinching
with a thousand times more power than you could foresee.

The crashendo ovation
to womanhood's beautiful, brutal performance.

A woman's power.

To carry all four seasons within her
and only show Spring.

To harness raging wildfire
and celestial tides
wrapped in earth-tone petal skin.

Out comes the needle and the thread
to sew up the carvings I didn't know I had.

"We had to cut you."
Please cut me all away next time
from head to toe.

Unfold me like a blanket
and leave me in the drawer under the bed
where it's dark and quiet and forgotten.

Bliss.

Grief is still grief
in a big, warm house.

But I'm grateful for that house

for the home that I made
to grow up in.

They tell me it's really over this time.

I've learned not to believe them,

I wish I could tell you they were right.

Through difficulty,
I learned that I can do difficult things.
That I can do important things.
That I can seemingly do anything.
That I can
and will
do whatever it takes
to do what's best
for me.

Gunshots of information:
Pounds, centimetres, circumference.

"But what does this mean..."
the girl inside whispers

Blood lost, length cut, drugs after drugs

"...how do I live now?"

It's time to get up, get workin', get knowin'

"Who will fix me?"

We are the healing healers, not they.
Through children's lives we do not pave our way.

The healing comes baked in to Sunday eggy bread
Warm drops of Christmas tree lights in our eyes
Listening to raw, unbridled anger
Taking the time to blow bubbles
Building cushion fortresses of routines

                                        - Don't just look at him,
                                              look at me

I brought home the bread
I put up those lights
I sheltered that anger
I blew bubbles until my hands froze
I built a fortress for, you, for me, for our whole world

I mother myself out of this trauma every day.
For we are the healing healers, not they.

I do the only thing I can
I call my mum.

Thank you, mum.

Thank you to every woman in my life who answered the call.

You are the lifeblood of this world.

# Postpartum

dread          dread
                     dread
          dread
dread     dread                    dread
          dread

dread I cower in the corner          dread  dread
          dread
     of the shower  dread     dread
dread
     turn my face away
dread and into the water     dread     dread
     dread

     away from my duties
away from the grief  dread  dread

dread

perpetually left unsaid                    dread
     dread

and evaporate into the white noise


that floods my head     dread          dread dread
          dread
dread     dread     dread
               dread  dread
               dread
dread               dread dread
dread                    dread
     dread
          dread
     dread                    dread
          dread

I saw him discover the wind
for the very first time
in this hair
as in the trees -
and he closes his eyes
to swim in the unfolding of his discovery
smiling in wonder.

"mamma, hear it?"

He takes my hand
and gifts me these first miracles
for no other reason than to share.

There aren't enough words to thank him.




"I hear it, baby. I hear it."

Any minute now
someone will help me get clean,
refreshed, hydrated, bring soft socks
and the smell of lavender.
Any minute now
someone will hand me a cup of tea,
no need to ask.
Any minute now
someone will use a quick wit to light the spark of laughter in me.
Any minute now
someone will teach me how to look after myself
and not just him.
Any minute now
someone will wrap me in a resolute hug
with a voice to match saying "That's enough. That's enough.
That's enough."
Any minute now
someone will ask me what happened
how are you?
how do you need to be?
Any minute now
someone will hold me,
lift me up away from all this,
save me.

Any minute now my people will arrive.

Any minute now.
Any minute now.

Though our voices may go quiet,
roots dormant under shifting lands,

when one of our own raises the call
we answer.

An ancient mighty forest faces the flames
to stand by a single tree.

Nothing,

nothing in this holy universe burns brighter,
more ferocious,
than womanhood called to arms.

What do we do
when we feel like we've run out of options?
No more options, no more body, no more.

                        Our

            souls

                    float

                            aimlessly,

                                    lost.

So we do what we're told.
It's better to be captured
by everyone else
than risk floating away
completely.

In the search to find my way back home
I learned to build my own

brick
by
brick

line by line.

I remember the exact moment
the switch went off
in that hospital bed
my eyes between the tiles.
And once the power fell from me
the parts of my body began to fall away too -
no magnetic core to hold it all together.

      I bled

         and I bled

            pulled clumps of tissue
                from out between my legs
as fast as the hair came away from my head
                  as my breasts became infected
             and rotted from the inside
              with skin so hot
                   it  p e e l e d  away
      like my stomach pulling
              down
             and away under the weight of
          falling and failing organs
carried on legs that can barely walk
or sit
or lie
because the pain was so much

I'm not fucking around when I say at times I thought I would die
lying in the pieces a body without a soul to hold it steady

    I    would    inevitably    fall    apart .

And all that shit
didn't make me stronger
but reminded me that any strength I have
is sometimes all that I have.

And all that shit
didn't mean I could handle anything
but that I must focus on being able to handle
whatever it is in the future, best I can

and stop worrying about losing my job
or my husband being unfaithful
or my friends moving on and away
or my family breaking apart
or my savings being lost
or my house being taken away

Because what I have
is all I have
And all that shit
didn't show me anything more
except that my world can keep shifting
but I am still my core.

Breast is best. Breast is best. Breast is best. Breast is best. Breast is best. Breast is best. Breast is best. Breast is best. Breast is best. Breast is best. Breast is best. Breast is best. Breast is best. Breast is best. Breast is best. Breast is best. Breast is best. Breast is best. Breast is best. Breast is best. Breast is best. Breast is best. Breast is best. Breast is best. Breast is best. Breast is best. Breast is best. Breast is best. Breast is best. Breast is best. Breast is best. Breast is best. Breast is best. Breast is best. Breast is best. Breast is best. Breast is best. Breast is best. Breast is best. Breast is best. Breast is best. Breast is best. Breast is best. Breast is best. Breast is best. Breast is best. Breast is best. Breast is best. Breast is best. Breast is best. Breast is best. Breast is best. Breast is best. Breast is best. Breast is best. Breast is best. Breast is best. Breast is best. Breast is best. Breast is best. Breast is best. Breast is best. Breast is best. Breast is best. Breast is best. Breast is best. Breast is best. Breast is best. Breast is best. Breast is best. Breast is best. Breast is best. Breast is best. Breast is best. Breast is best. Breast is best. Breast is best. Breast is best. Breast is best. Breast is best. Breast is best. Breast is best. Breast is best. Breast is best. Breast is best. Breast is best. Breast is best. Breast is best. Breast is best. Breast is best. Breast is best. Breast is best. Breast is best. Breast is best. Breast is best. Breast is best. Breast is best. Breast is best. Breast is best. Breast is best. Breast is best. Breast is best. Breast is best. Breast is best. Breast is best. Breast is best. Breast is best. Breast is best. Breast is best. Breast is best. Breast is best. Breast is best. Breast is best. Breast is best. Breast is best. Breast is best. Breast is best. Breast is best. Breast is best. Breast is best. Breast is best. Breast is best. Breast is best. Breast is best. Breast is best. Breast is best. Breast is best. Breast is best. Breast is best. Breast is best. Breast is best. Breast is best. Breast is best. Breast is best. Breast is best. Breast is best. Breast is best. Breast is best. Breast is best. Breast is best. Breast is best. Breast is best. Breast is best. Breast is best. Breast is best. Breast is best. Breast is best. Breast is best. Breast is best. Breast is best. Breast is best. Breast is best. Breast is best. Breast is best. Breast is best. Breast is best. Breast is best. Breast is best. Breast is best. Breast is best. Breast is best. Breast is best. Breast is best. Breast is best. Breast is best. Breast is best. Breast is best. Breast is best. Breast is best. Breast is best. Breast is best. Breast is best. Breast is best. Breast is best. Breast is best. Breast is

Breastmilk isn't the centre of your baby's universe.

You are.

Cocoon myself in exhaustion
as they unbutton my shirt.
They take my breasts to feed him
and an echo of an old voice questions

"Is this meant to hurt?"

Just bunker down, honey.
They don't need you to be conscious
to do your job.

There was no specialist breastfeeding support
But oh there's a consultant for that

There was no opportunity for sleep
But oh there's lots of courses for that

There was no psychologist to help us
But oh there's private ones for that

There was no reassurance in your decisions
But oh there's online clubs of ideologies for that

There was no procedure of postpartum trauma
But oh there's self-help books for that

There was no space for self-care
But oh there's always a product for that

Stop selling new mums the shit they don't need
and if it's shit that they really need, then they should get it
for free.

When we're broken and tired and desperate for help they sell us
principles and programs and goddamn fucking product after
product.

You deserve better than that.

I wanted this baby so badly.
I wanted this life more than I can say.

But right now,
right in this moment
I just need to be held.
And for everything else to be taken away.

I am still the main character
of my life
she reminded herself.

Music is canonised and curated just for me.
The snow falls in slow motion to suspend the scenery at my feet.
And summer storms flood in with pathetic fallacy at my conductive
emotional whim.

Time bends around my trauma and triumphs.
Only my laughter causes the ripples around these eyes.

I hold the red thread
of everything I've known.

Through my skin
the tapestry of experience
is sewn.

My coincidences are poetry
each moment a rhythm for a rhyme.
I will support, with passion, the main plot for others.
But the only story I'll ever have is mine.

A baby suffers from hunger
in a hospital in Norway.

A hospital
In Norway
A baby suffers from hunger

because you say it's not good enough.

Let's pause on that
like the mamma's have done every single day since.

Only then
in fever
from hunger
do you bring out their drink
from under lock and key
portion it out into tiny cups
don't you dare ask for more
don't. you. dare.

A mamma leaves the hospital
not knowing how to feed her baby

but still, you tell her it wasn't good enough.

It's good enough.

All of my water runs red now.
Feet drowning in life that I didn't consent to drain

and my heart sinks down with it all.
A life stained.

I silently slip down
melting away
in the heat.

In still and silent soil
a garden grows its roots.

Run to the bathroom
cradle the blood clot, two hands,
out from my pyjama leg
lay the evidence in the shower
weep and bleed the rest of me into the toilet
cry out for my mother
as my own life drains from me.

And she was still there
to wash my soiled clothes
to bring me tea without ask
to cry on my behalf
to rage in equal part
to carry him when I couldn't
at times she carried all of us


before getting back on that plane


my biggest witness in the dark days
a shooting star in flight.

From the moment we bleed,
we bleed wrong.

An imposter in my life and body
no more.

The secret to defeating imposter syndrome?
Allowance.

Allow yourself to just show up
Allow what comes naturally to come.
Allow space for things to happen.

And when they do,
allow them to be perfect and imperfect
all the same.

Without imposition there is no imposter,
only you.

The poison and the pain
in my chest
grew so large
it burst from my skin
left me permanently scarred

but because "pain is normal"
I didn't. even. notice.
as my bra filled with blood
and puss
I kept on rocking him to sleep
sang the songs in a darling sweet hush

no more cries

not his nor mine.

If anyone knows
the difference between pain
and suffering,
it's women.

Right now
as you read this

she is laid out
strapped down
all alone in 1 of 100 hospital beds.

Battered
bleeding
with a poisoned, bandaged chest.

She would sob silently
had there been worth in her tears.

Instead, she lies latent
and languid.

Abandoned by the society
that pushed her there for years.

But my heart is with her
in that lonely world of one.
And weeps on her behalf,
always.

After the infection exploded out
through shotgun holes in my skin
the doctor at the hospital revered
"Isn't the human body amazing?"

What body?
Oh. That one there.
The one I used to call

Me.

In the shape of a body.
In the shape of a body she shelters.
In the shape of a body she lies.
In the shape of a body she moves through her life with whatever
decorum or dominance that she bloody well likes.
In the shape of a body she holds children.
In the shape of a body she governs men.
In the shape of a body she is denounced and disturbed
but this body is built for her, not for them.
She moves through them.
In the shape of a body she escapes.
In the shape of a body she builds a well.
In the shape of a body she layers on muscle and mail and art
and thick rugged bark
and everything she needs for her monarchel shell.

A senior doctor
at the clinic
took a picture
with her phone
of my exposed
and bloody chest.

Without telling me why
Without saying a word

I never thought
to even ask
because by then
I'd already abandoned
my self
my respect
in their ward.

I'm so sorry that happened to you.

And there are wards of us, you know.

Imagine.
Just imagine
if we had as much indignant rage
about wealth inequality
as we do about breastfeeding.

When you cut inside me
and sweep me out
please just take the rest.
Take out the womb
that belongs to the world
take out what used to be my breasts
sew up the pussy
shave my head
for fuck sake whatever it takes,
to allow me to rest.

Stress is physical.
Stress is physical.
Stress is physical.
Stress is physical.
Stress is physical.
Stress is physical.
Stress is physical.
Stress is physical.
Stress is physical.
Stress is physical.
Stress is physical.
Stress is physical.
Stress is physical.
Stress is physical.
Stress is physical.
Stress is physical.
Stress is physical.
Stress is physical.
Stress is physical.
Stress is physical.
Stress is physical.
Stress is physical.
Stress is physical.
Stress is physical.
Stress is physical.
Stress is physical.
Stress is physical.
Stress is physical.
Stress is physical.
Stress is physical.
Stress is physical.
Stress is physical.
Stress is physical.
Stress is physical.
Stress is physical.
Stress is physical.
Stress is physical.

I leave such a sour taste
on the tongues of mothers
who see my blood
as stains on us all.

Maybe it isn't what's different or better
about me and her
but about the cards we drew.

Maybe it was hard for her
but not as hard.
Maybe she has family close
a child who slept
who was easily fed
a different career
or none at all
a luckier birth
or an easier postpartum
less socialisation to be the absolute "perfect" mum.
A nanny
frequent sitters
fuck it
no wonder my grief tastes sharp
and bitter.

Maybe her home
like her life
had a little more space
and it's not me
but my circumstances
that were a little out of place.

Slam my body
with sobs
against the shower tiles.

"This isn't what I wanted!"
I yell against the water
pouring out soul
with my blood
down to the earth.

        The thinnest glass door,
        the only one I can hide behind.

"I don't want this."
I confess on my knees
hoping someone higher than me will respond
and take the unbearable away.

        But they don't.

So I step out of my glass confessional
to the sounds of his commands

wrap myself tight in the empress's clothes
and extend out my arms
empty of any hope or prayers
to make room for his.

It takes a spine of spider silk
to stand upright in quicksand


carrying a weight that keeps on growing
just like you dreamed it would.

Mid sentence here, my one-year-old wakes with a cough
and a cry.

There's a molten core inside of her body
that lifts her to her feet,

*(VY  CMa)*

towards that cry,
towards that cough,
that thud,
or a silence only she can hear,
before her muscles even know she's moving.

Away from these pages,
into his room,
into his cry, to take it for him.

The heaviness we haul,
day in and day out.
Carried on delicate whispers of song, feather-light smiles,
tiny kisses on their forehead.
Scaffolding around a raging furness,
smoky,
made of Sheffield steel.

We continue on, but never from where we left off.

We continue on, but never from where we left off.

I need to learn how to love us both
but there's still so much to do.
The only love I ever learned
was to graft

# and give
# and give

so I'll give it all to you.

The little things become big things.

The people in our arms,
what they're capable of,
the steps we take together.

The stillness after chaos,
quiet moments in between,
the warmth of your tea.

The taste of the ocean in seafood,
the pop of wine corks,
large tables with matching dessert forks.

Laughing until you cry,
being able to cry at all,
the hugs that linger just a little.

Sleep.

A cat on your lap,
none of us rushed to move,
seeing trees outside your window.

The muscles on your back,
the broadness of your shoulders,
all the ambitions you dare to carry.

They grow
and we grow
and the value of our time grows too.

The little things become big things.

All day, every day. All day, every day. All day, every day. All day, every day. All day, every day. All day, every day. All day, every day. All day, every day. All day, every day. All day, every day. All day, every day. All day, every day. All day, every day. All day, every day. All day, every day. All day, every day. All day, every day. All day, every day. All day, every day. All day, every day. All day, every day. All day, every day. All day, every day. All day, every day. All day, every day. All day, every day. All day, every day. All day, every day. All day, every day. All day, every day. All day, every day. All day, every day. All day, every day. All day, every day. All day, every day. All day, every day. All day, every day. All day, every day. All day, every day. All day, every day. All day, every day. All day, every day. All day, every day. All day, every day. All day, every day. All day, every day. All day, every day. All day, every day. All day, every day. All day, every day. All day, every day. All day, every day. All day, every day. All day, every day. All day, every day. All day, every day. All day, every day. All day, every day. All day, every day. All day, every day. All day, every day. All day, every day. All day, every day. All day, every day. All day, every day. All day, every day. All day, every day. All day, every day. All day, every day. All day, every day. All day, every day. All day, every day. All day, every day. All day, every day. All day, every day. All day, every day. All day, every day. All day, every day. All day, every day. All day, every day. All day, every day. All day, every day. All day, every day. All day, every day. All day, every day. All day, every day. All day, every day. All day, every day. All day, every day. All day, every day. All day, every day. All day, every day. All day, every day. All day, every day. All day, every day. All day, every day. All day, every day. All day, every day.

Sharpen your sword,
protect your peace.

Space.

Oh god, please grant me space.

Forced to live in tiny squares
of homes,
and roles,
and check-boxes.

I rebel into a place of my own
balancing whimsically between the edges of paper

I create endless space
borderless and free
but wholly, fucking mine.

You can squash and confine
and barricade us
I dare you.
Forced to look inwards, we bravely face
in to our radical,
limitless
power.

Exhaustion is
syphoning away the person
to fill a body

with dead-weight cement
to sustain our poise
in the constant storm.

Patience is
my act of defiance
against the lore
that time is earned,
not lived.

My rebellion
to reclaim the ground
beneath my feet,
to breathe,
to feel,
to boldly be.

Not good enough?

Nurses had to hold me down
as they pulled infection from my breasts
and I screamed like a frightened child

     but still, you told me it wasn't good enough.

So I bite down on cotton cloths instead
trying not to yell
fuck
shit
cunt
as he latches and I grip his precious newborn head,

     but still, you told me it wasn't good enough.

In fleeting rations of feverish rest
I wake in sweat and hallucinate
that there's a dying baby on my chest

     but still, you told me it wasn't good enough.

Rushed to hospital far from him,
taped, tubed, injected, stitched, and bruised
because god forbid the fucking milk runs thin

       but still,
       you told me
       it wasn't good enough.

I didn't fail,
I was failed.

It takes a village.

I thought I only needed me and you -

and in the gap

between us                                                    and the others

I lost you too.

We had such little money, back then
but you still took me to Paris
and on the last day we spent our final pennies
on fancy little macarons
in the poshest pastry box and matching bag.
The poshest I'd ever seen.
We carried that bag like the people on postcards
advertising the perfect life.
We made so many plans didn't we?
About when we would eat them
share and savour each bite
together.
Let's keep the champagne flavour for our anniversary
but have the truffle and vanilla ones when you visit me next.
When we see each other again.
We always had to plan for that.
Until we got to Charles de Gaulle
and in the chaos and the vastness and the goodbyes
we forgot the macarons!
God, how we kicked ourselves
but laughed so hard at our slipup.
How classic, silly and daydreamy we were.
We reminisced about that story for years
until the story became sweeter than those little macarons
and I know we'll be sharing it
someday again, when we're really old.

I like to imagine
that posh little bag
of silly little macarons
is still sat at Charles de Gaulle.
A permanent memorial
of an old, young love that we savour.

I swallow requests on rote,
gulp them down "one day at a time"
like thick, sticky medicine.
Good girl, good girl,
I learn never to make a fuss.

But the boundaries in my throat are bursting,
lungs gorged with words I hoard.
A breath would taste so good right now
but I'm stuck.
Stuck rigidly in this stance my lungs know.

So,
I swallow my exhaustion on rote.
Good girl until the end.
Filling myself with the right thing to do,
only to discover
it's not medicine, it's glue.

I buckle him in to take him to nursery.
My heart grows every time I put on his helmet
and he winces a little, but let's me anyway,
those big, little moments of bravery.
I give my own a knock
to show him I've got mine too.

I close the transparent shield,
climb up high on to my pedals
and away we go.

The world opens and expands right in front of me,
like it just opened its mouth for the biggest breath
it has taken in decades
and I engulf that shared breath like famished flame in hay.

The view is so good from up here.

God,
tastes so sweet
and for some moments I am her ...

I cut from everything I have
Drove my hands into the dirt
Rinse, repeat
and slashed away more.
100 glass jars from window to door.

I nurtured, tendered
and grew so much life
in a frantic attempt
to experience a feeling
that I would have no more.

... My boy exclaims in delight
at the cars and the buses and the big green bin lorry
and sometimes I respond
and sometimes I don't
sometimes I let the river take my attention instead
or the inertia in the bends
or the gift of realising I can taste what it feels like
to be alive again.

His wistful, peaceful breaths
wake me from sleep

like bombs.

Step into the dark,
look under the bed,
seek out the real monsters
that live in your head.

Our mother tongue is martyrdom
inquiries about our needs don't translate.

I cannot answer without the words
I was never taught to speak.

I need.
I want.
I won't.

The voice that says
I need
I want
I won't

is an echo
of a soul that knows
she deserves.

She may be quiet now
but she is there.

As a child I patched my bones
with a needle and thread.
Stitched myself stable
with an armour of lead.

And now I'm so full
and these bones are so heavy,
I can barely get out of bed.
The weight of it all
is too much to carry.

Until the taste of poison
becomes unbearably strong,
I bite down,
grind out some more
and patch up my bones
again
and again,
to obligations' siren song.

All this time
I thought motherhood broke me
but it was the breaking of my childhood stories all along

So watch me now
as I raise us both
in the wisdom
of what it really means
to be strong.

There are enough hours in the day
but none of them are mine.

It wasn't more time that I needed
but more choice
to do with time
what I needed
to make it mine.

We exist
on rations of silent,
tiny breaths.

Fluttering by
so mechanically
as if we barely breathe at all.


And they treat us as such.

When was the last time
you
goddamn
filled
your
lungs?

Saturate yourself
with as much
delicious,
dazzling,
electric air
that you can drink.

It's here


that we forge
a sparkling,
supernatural oasis
from which the most tyrannical sand dunes
will melt at our feet.

I don't know where I should be
I just know it isn't here -
and every drink takes me further away.

Bittersweet sips
that taste deceptively like freedom.

I retire my soul
to the scriptorium that I built
and draw out all the maps I ever needed
on papyrus paper

and diligently tear them up and fold them
and fold them
and fold them
super small
under your fingernails small.

I go back in time
and enshrine them one by one
as a buried paper trail
for the me
that needed them then.

I'll leave these crumbs of parchment
in cheesy Halloween decorations, in fingerpaint murals, in the
unfurled picnic blanket that we lay on the living room floor.
In Chinese takeout boxes, in the pictures we didn't remember to
take, in glasses of Oyster Bay.
In my husband's guitar strings, in the bird foot under his cuff, in the
fine lines that I loved to hold in his hands.
In blue dotted paper, in the most breathtaking books,
in lemon and ginger tea.
And it won't be until years later
when these crumbs of paper
tie into reams
and the reams become the walls
and the door
to the scriptorium that I built for my soul.

I desperately cling to old photographs
but I do not recognise your face.

I anchor myself
to the freckle in the middle of my collar bones.
When everything else is lost to insanity
that fragment of me is always there.

I try to see you.
To really see you.
But there's a screen between us.
Floating shapes trapped in our eyes that disappear
- they pass through without a mark.

How can a mother forget her son's face?


Can you see the glass between us?
The haze that distances us.
Can you feel it too?

Fuck, I'm so so sorry.

He looks to the bright sky.
Excited for the moon he cannot see.

Just knowing there is beauty out there
brings him joy.

It's not the screams that hurt me,
the tiny fists that slam
or those stubborn little legs that kick and thump and thrash.

What hurts is the adult voice inside my head
reminding me

"you deserve this."

The voice inside my head...

...Whose voice is that?

She craves sleep,
- this deep hunger -

but fears waking
the next day.

So she shuns sleep,
- this veiled poison -

and just like that,
she starves.

And every night
I use what little breath I have
on the most important words I'll ever say
"I love you"
"I love you"
"I love you"
"I love you"

"I'm tired." "I'm tired." "I'm tired." "I'm tired." "I'm tired." "I'm tired." "I'm tired." "I'm tired." "I'm tired." "I'm tired." "I'm tired." "I'm tired." "I'm tired." "I'm tired." "I'm tired." "I'm tired." "I'm tired." "I'm tired." "I'm tired." "I'm tired." "I'm tired." "I'm tired." "I'm tired." "I'm tired." "I'm tired." "I'm tired." "I'm tired." "I'm tired." "I'm tired." "I'm tired." "I'm tired." "I'm tired." "I'm tired." "I'm tired." "I'm tired." "I'm tired." "I'm tired." "I'm tired." "I'm tired." "I'm tired." "I'm tired." "I'm tired." "I'm tired." "I'm tired." "I'm tired." "I'm tired." "I'm tired." "I'm tired." "I'm tired." "I'm tired." "I'm tired." "I'm tired." "I'm tired." "I'm tired." "I'm tired." "I'm tired." "I'm tired." "I'm tired." "I'm tired." "I'm tired." "I'm tired." "I'm tired." ("I'm lost") "I'm tired." "I'm tired." "I'm tired." "I'm tired." "I'm tired." "I'm tired." "I'm tired." "I'm tired." "I'm tired." "I'm tired." "I'm tired." "I'm tired." "I'm tired." "I'm tired." "I'm tired." "I'm tired." "I'm tired." "I'm tired." "I'm tired." "I'm tired." "I'm tired."  "I'm tired." "I'm tired." "I'm tired." "I'm tired." "I'm tired." "I'm tired." "I'm tired." "I'm tired." "I'm tired." "I'm tired." "I'm tired." "I'm tired." "I'm tired." "I'm tired." "I'm tired." "I'm tired." "I'm tired." "I'm tired." "I'm tired." "I'm tired." "I'm tired." "I'm tired." "I'm tired." "I'm tired." "I'm tired." "I'm tired." "I'm tired." "I'm tired." "I'm tired." "I'm tired." "I'm tired." "I'm tired." "I'm tired." "I'm tired." "I'm tired." "I'm tired." "I'm tired." "I'm tired." "I'm tired." "I'm tired." "I'm tired." "I'm tired." "I'm tired." "I'm tired." "I'm tired." "I'm tired."

She had the audacity
to pursue rituals purely for joy.

Away from curation
currency
and content.

And in these moments
where all other eyes were turned away

She turned up
turned it on
and found her way.

I lived under the cheap glow of the microwave clock
that still singes the edges of my eyes
all these years later.

For every time someone told me
to "enjoy every precious moment"
I
would
lose
myself
in
weeks.

There is no light at the end of the tunnel
no end in sight at all.
But every moment that I breathe
I move forward in time
regardless.

Regardless of the heaviest weight
and soul-scathing thoughts

I don't know what's at the end of the tunnel
but as long as I breathe
I will get there.

And like we've been taught for thousands of years;
we sit in circles,
the songs begin
but the melodies and movements are new and foreign to me.

I try my best to keep rhythm
making up for my mistakes
with water smiles
and big well eyes.

But I falter
again and again
and I let you down.

Vi sitter
et øyeblikk
på grener av klossete ord

men lever
i den stille luften mellom dem

svever harmonisk

i vårt tause sjelespråk.

Heavy and disgusting.

A body dipped, like candle wax
in layers of blood and sweat.

The core of me felt impossible to clean
so I burned it away from the inside instead.

Motherhood wasn't as hard on me
as I was on myself.

We give grace.
We give home.

We give life.
We give blood.

And the world teaches us
it's never enough.

Sometimes the story is simply this:

A shitty thing happened
(that shouldn't have)
and now you're showing up
to the shitty work
to move through
the shitty feelings.

And that's that.

You carried my secrets
before you could walk.

Witnessed your mamma's sobs
in bathroom stalls
on laundry piles
silent reverbs in the nursery halls.

Curated in silence
just for one;

the heaviest of secrets
held between

us                     two.

and now I look back
at the time we both learned to walk.

Holding on to each other
through our beautiful
devastating
growth.

How is it possible
to be willing to die for someone
that I struggle to give my life to?

We give them life
but our own is ours alone.

Always has been.
Always will be.

Belonging with them
not to them.

All that force has to go somewhere.
Something has to give.


The smile on rote,
the job we hate,
the people that suck. us. dry.
The push and shove
of the avalanche of days.
A crack in the dam.
Can't take it anymore.
Stronger than I ever knew
but with skin stretched so thin.


                              Something has to give.
                        Nothing suffocates forever.




                        Nothing suffocates forever.

The future is
not mine to hold,
through grasping I do try.
With frenzied hands
I weave intricate plans.
My frayed intentions
forced through discontent's steely eye.

Then,
through tragedy or triumph,
a great unravelling I will allow.
From these hands
strung a heart that understands
I can live forever
in the timeless,
expansive,
completeness of now.

Trauma doesn't change us,
it fractures the world we're in.

And we break ourselves
into        jagged,
                    sticky
                            pieces

to frantically fill,
secure,
and fix that world.

Maybe I didn't hate being a mum,
                I just hated myself.

Maybe I didn't lose myself to motherhood,
                I just lost myself.

Maybe it wasn't the worst thing that happened,
                maybe I just couldn't see
                what was happening at all.


Maybe.


Just maybe.

# Depression

Betrayed by the nightmare
that I had longed for
as human-scent dreams.

# RUTH ROSTRUP

I use my shame
to bleach the grief

as my partner scrubs our pregnancy
from the sofa.

I dream of fetuses
babies
and a child
lined up in a blood-soaked bath
and I'm told to choose
where I'd like to fail next.

Paralysed by the reality
of all the life
and death
my own body is forsaken to carry.

# RUTH ROSTRUP

So excuse me if I'm a little weary or distracted
there's a century of women's pain
behind these winged lines.

Where women learn to keep it tucked away,
concealing the ancient shadows in our eyes.

RUTH ROSTRUP

An immigrant
in motherhood.

I live between
and feel far from
two separate homes.

The life before and the life after.
Performing on tandem ropes I balance between -

Between two languages I'll never really master,
two cultures I'll never understand,
two versions of a life I'll never fully experience.

A foreigner in both.

On dotted paper
I write down my desires
and my dreams.
Formulating my heart's reality in blotched, inky streams.


And I try to calculate how motherhood equates to this.

But from every angle, it never adds up,
the numbers just aren't right.

I'm suffocating in the impossibility.

She walked to the midwives, babe in arms
they contradicted
they gaslit
they dismissed her

She walked to the doctors, babe in arms
they misdiagnosed
they wrongly prescribed
they dismissed her

She walked to the gynaecologist, babe in arms
they mistook
they forgot
they dismissed her

She walked to the clinic, babe in arms
they scarred
they mistreated
they dismissed her

She walked to the psychologist, babe in arms
they berated
they coerced
they dismissed her

She walked to the community nurses, babe in arms
told them she couldn't carry on no more
they told her to sing
they told her to smile
and they dismissed her

So she walked to the edge of the cliff, empty arms
empty body
she dismissed her own cries for help
and walked into the emptiness instead.

# Ruth Rostrup

The harder I work
the better I'll be

yet here I am,
sick and tired.

So I'll work some more

to be a better mum
a better daughter
a better worker
a better woman

even though
the "better" I work
the sicker I become.

Why is it that every time I step up, my body shuts down?

And I realise I'm dying
yet I'm not afraid, I'm relieved
maybe then
I'll give myself permission to rest in peace
after I die in the most worthy way.
Working.
Crafting.
The sacrificial warrior woman.

She used to sing.

The melodies are trapped
in chained-up shoulders
padlocked and welded
to her hostage ears.

# Ruth Rostrup

Stress cascades from my crown
into my body
fills me up
overflows my cup
as I pass it around
asking what else I can take
while my insides drown
and rusts
and rots away.
But I steady my hands
with the sceptre and cup
and gaze tearfully over my kingdom
knowing it may kill me
but for them
I'll never give up.

She rises
and she falls
in the shadow
of the master of swords.

She is a tornado-
An unstoppable, unconscious force of chaos
encapsulating a mute, silent core.


I tear forcefully through days
and tasks
and people.
Futilely fleeing from the scars I trail behind me.

The chaos fuels my chaos
until I burn myself out.

Every day I wash the dishes
but today I let my hands unfold
at the bottom of the sink

I let the warm, bubbly water
embrace them
and me

as my shoulders dip in a ripple with them

and I weep

in the safest embrace I have felt in months.

Giant, rough, intruder hands
slam into my chest
and smother my face to the wall

I shrink and sob
behind a placid, cool glass face
"Please, please, just take what you want."

at the tissue hands
and feather voice
of the young child patting my leg for a hug.

I was painting our lives
layer after layer
and as the canvas grew
so did the buckets
lifting brush after brush
heavy and thick
my eyes swim through the task
until I could just about drown
in the richness of the image
I wanted us to live in.

But the more layers I added
the more cracks did form
so I added some more
until our yellow turned brown
and the greens bled to black.

How many years did I lose to the colourful cover-up?

I drown in colours, like tar, that never seem to sit.

Another child?

Pfft. Fuck that.
No way.
I don't get it at all.

Crazy.

I don't know how you're even considering it.

How can you do that?

How?

Tell me.

Please.

Oh God, please tell me how.

RUTH ROSTRUP

I'm fine. No, really, I'm feeling pretty good! Things seem to be getting better. I'm definitely on the way up. Wow, yeh, maybe this is it. I'm out of the thick of it and starting to get better. The world does look good today. I haven't cried in days. This feels good. All of the dark days are behind me now. Yeh, yeh things are going well! I can't complain really. I think I'm better y'know. I'm alright! Yeh, good, thanks for asking.

I'm grand. I'm feeling good. Yeh things are great. I'm OK. Really. I'm fine. I'm fine. I'm fine. I'm fine. Oh fuck. What's happening? Oh no. No. I'm not OK. I'm really not OK.

A beautiful scene plays out.
Pappa and his boy
sharing stories only they will know
over sweet porridge, milk and firelight.

I smell the warmth,
taste their laughter.

I want to take you there
but I can't.

I watch, not through a screen
but through a door
I should be able to step through,
but I don't.

I can't blame heavy bedsheets.

They're my play pretend paper shield.

You hear my silent sadness
between the lullabies
and I see a stillness come over you
between the coos and cries.

We share a moment of ageless understanding

as I pour my sadness
into your wide, absorbent eyes.

In low light
the smallest people
can cast the biggest shadow.

# Ruth Rostrup

I stand in the snow
outside your window
and weep in the shadow of our door.

To step inside would mean being crushed
in rooms, and things, and days that are weeks that are years.

I freeze
homeless
in the doorway
of my home.

As the longing to be with and without brutally tears me in two.

I wish I could remember
your soft little snores
as much as the stitches, the soreness and burns.

I wish I could remember
your honey satin skin
as much as the blood, sweat and never feeling clean.

I wish I could remember
those cute little hiccups
as much as the fucked up breastfeeding and painful pumps.

I wish I could remember
those enchanting newborn eyes
as much as the panic attacks night after night after goddam night.

I wish I would have remembered
both you and me.

# RUTH ROSTRUP

Every day I push that stroller
up along the edge of the fjord.

My perfect content little baby
in our expensive, matching clothes
sing-song voices
and warm smiles for strangers.

Overlooking the richest city in the world.

The whole while contemplating
what would be the cost
of my only two options -

Leave my baby at the edge of the cliff
or take him over with me.

I pack your tiny blankets in the drawer,
fold up the memories,
pretend that they're weightless
just because they're small.

I wrap the colour and softness
in airtight plastic and tape.
Put my daydreams into storage
and hide the evidence of expectations
I was silly enough to make.

And when all is empty and silent,
a terror in me does arise.
My mouth fills with chlorine
as I hear
buried under blankets and bags
a newborn's desperate cries.

In the dark, unable to breathe.
Oh God please don't be true.
In my selfish desperation
to bury all of our pain
did I suffocate you too?

I rip open all the bags
and tear into the drawer,
cover the room in chaos and sobs
to find you're not there,
it's just me.
Surrounded
suffocated
and small.

I crave the sound
of summer rain

but never listen
when she arrives.

Burnout
dug a hole in my depression
so deep
that I couldn't hear my anxiety any longer.
They were still there of course
razer sharp ripples cutting through the cells of my organs-
But I heard no screams.

For the first time in my life there was silence.

I heard, felt and experienced nothing.
I became nothing.
Is this peace?
All this time I was searching for home
to find my quiet
and here I am in the bottom of the deepest hole of my life
encompassed in a place so peaceful
I don't even care
that I'm so far from home
and even as my colleagues
and my friends
and my family
and my lover
and my child
and my body
cry out
I keep dig
dig
digging away
not out of stubbornness
or delusion
or drive
but out of nothingness.

There is an absence in me
that is so loud
and so heavy.

I lost my sanity
to the tune of my own lullabies.

Dear friend,

~~How are you?~~

~~What's going on with~~

~~We should get together and~~

I have so much I want to say to you but where do I start?

I guess that became the problem.

I couldn't keep up. It's hard to admit but I couldn't keep up and you left me behind.

And I mean it sincerely when I say that's genuinely fine.

Behind my shame I just want you to be happy, to live your life, prioritise your energy and time.

From where I stood our friendship wasn't bound by texts or calls or check-ins

so I thought it would be ok if that unravelled.

But we're not in each other's shoes and now we're so far away.

I guess I hoped it was just a beautiful chapter coming naturally to its end,

rather than your own story of me turning into the shameful tragedy that I failed you.

That I was a bad friend.

I constantly write out and then delete apologies in my head, for being shit, for not showing up, for not being enough.

But I can't send that to you. Because it would mean that if I could go back I'd do it a different way. I'd give you more.

But I know that isn't true.

I was giving everything I had to just fucking survive and if I'm being really honest with you, which I hope we can still be, I still get struck by the miracle that I'm even alive.

Yes, you absolutely deserved better and for fuck sake so did I. I guess I just hoped

when I was able to make it through again you'd be there on the other side.

The voice of my fractured heart
breaks yours,
so I'll keep it to myself.

I keep a bag packed
in the hidden corner
of my mind

just in case.

Or if the time comes
I'm ready
to go make myself safe
in a world of people who keep moving away.

Why do we daydream
of cabins
and forests
but never go?

I say
I'm afraid I'll never come back.

He replies
you've already gone.

I write myself out over and over again
just to convince myself of
or remember
who I am.

The person before the feeling came.

But every day it spills out onto my pages
until none of my sentences make any sense.

And I try to find the words to describe myself
in skills
and tasks
and time spent
on actions that are supposed to speak louder than words.

Hey you,

There's enough sorrow here.
I'll soak it up for all of us.

And when my body is saturated
I'll sink to the bottom of the lake
and watch your storybook boats,
carried on ripples of laughter
that I'm too far down to touch.

I interlace my fingers
in the chain mail sand
and become the water.
The child I love is on my shore,
I'll wash away his sorrow too.

The nethermost dark, reflecting only light.

Be everything, become nothing. No more.

*I see you now.*

My life sentence writes itself out by the second.

and I constantly wonder
what's more terrifying;

an incomplete sentence
or one that's met its end.

And I'm really sorry
that you went through what you did.

Getting things in order
to say goodbye
can look a lot like
getting better.

*I wish I could go back,*

*scoop you up,*

*hug you in,*

*and take you away from all that.*

I leave my body in the company of others
and slip away
into a blanket of quiet.

The banter and laughter of friends
that once woke my soul

becomes the muffled buzzing of a TV left on
in the background of a kids sleepover;
you drift off to the plot of a film that fades away.

Did time freeze or flutter by?
Was it in my safety or solace
or overwhelm
that my eyes glazed over.

You ask
"Hey, are you ok?"
"Yeh, I'm just tired"
a voice replies, that sounds like mine.

*But the best I can do*
*is want that for you*
*because you deserve better.*
*You deserve so, so much better.*

An innocent, heaven-scent
descendent of snow
collapses a sacred tree
of a hundred winters carried.

Snaps her back.
Smothers her lungs.
buries her in alluring, deadly silence.

The last thing she carries
is her liberated breath
that sighs to the sky
"finally."

If I were you
I'd cry too.
I'd cry tears so hot and so angry
they'd tear right through the other side.

Life wasn't taken from me
I let it all go

Bled away the warmth
to stop the tides of pain

Shrunk myself to nothing
to relieve the pressure
of trying to be everything.

The other side of all this bullshit,

this pain,

this exhaustion.

Sometimes I wonder
if the only reason I didn't take my own life
was because I became incapable
of taking anything for myself at all.

The hardest thing
you'll ever carry with you.
I promise, it is.

She holds up oceans in her sleep
wakes in sweat,
drowned in heat.

Saved the world
but at what cost?

We'll never know.

Under heavy nights,
steeped in terror
she is lost.

And fuck all the advice,
there's nothing more you need to do.

**Don't** touch me.
Don't **touch** me.
Don't touch **me.**

*You are enough.*

*You were always enough.*

The only thing I hated more
than my experience
was me.

Just promise me this;
Keep showing up
for yourself.

My greenhouse body
absorbs grief
through glass skin and bones of tin.

I paint my walls with flowers
to hide the rotting earth within.

One moment at a time,

one line at a time,

one line at a time.

I will carry your shadow
for the rest of my days.

Long after the flowers have returned to their home,
like the guests who busied on to my shoreline
with buckets and mops
only to return to their own.

And after the avalanche
of texts and tears and check-ins
have settled

I will stand in the vastness of this stark reality -
A life
carved out and crushed
by the absence of you.

I will carry your shadow
for the rest of my days.

As bills drop slyly back onto the doormat
and work drips meetings into my time
and family drops vacuuming, dishes and pans
and hope drips recklessly into my plans
as all the dropped balls find their way
to my hands.

drip, drip, drip, drop
The world relentlessly pours on.

But then, when I need,
I'll retreat into your shadow.
Into the deep, the dark, the quiet.
The solace I cultivated in the greatest of loss.
In a refuge, I will carry for the rest of my days.

Keep writing out your story.

This is yours.

To do with as you need,

as you want,

as you are,

no more.

# Created, with love, by Ruth Rostrup

during baby nap times, late nights after long workdays, on tram
rides, in airports and midnight notes on a mobile phone
- the small solitary moments where we can learn to dream big again.

# Edited by Leah Plotz

who skilfully nurtured the small details, often with one hand, while
cradling a newborn in the other.
You are magnificent.

# Thank you

to the international mothers who gifted their words for page 36.
Connecting with you is a gift in itself.

Amina Ibrahim

Claudia Menger

R. Skjerven

Izabella Katharina Abouradoine Sætherø

Iina Zischka

Tatiana Shcherbakova

Elzevera Albada Jelgersma

Olga Pietruszka

and to Wigdis Watnedalen
my mother-in-law
who helped me perch more confidently on page 209
(and generally in my life in Norway)

and my husband Even,
the best life teammate I could wish for.

# Support and share

✤ Gift me to the people you love

✤ Leave a review on Amazon

✤ Share the words
@RuthRostrup #MoreTheBook